T0035810

Into the Deep!

by Maria Le
illustrations by Alison Hawkins

Ready-to-Read

SIMON SPOTLIGHT
An imprint of Simon & Schuster Children's Publishing Division
New York   London   Toronto   Sydney   New Delhi
1230 Avenue of the Americas, New York, New York 10020
This Simon Spotlight edition May 2023
Text copyright © 2023 by Simon & Schuster, Inc.
Illustrations copyright © 2023 by Alison Hawkins • Stock photos by iStock
All rights reserved, including the right of reproduction in whole or in part in any form.
SIMON SPOTLIGHT, READY-TO-READ, and colophon are registered trademarks of Simon & Schuster, Inc.
For information about special discounts for bulk purchases, please contact Simon & Schuster Special Sales at
1-866-506-1949 or business@simonandschuster.com.
Manufactured in the United States of America 0323 LAK
2 4 6 8 10 9 7 5 3 1
This book has been cataloged by the Library of Congress.
ISBN 978-1-6659-3356-8 (pbk)
ISBN 978-1-6659-3357-5 (hc)
ISBN 978-1-6659-3358-2 (ebook)

Glossary

adapt: to become suited to a particular situation

bioluminescent: having light produced by living organisms

biosphere: the part of the world in which life can exist

ecosystem: a network of organisms and their environment functioning as a unit

filter feeders: animals that filter food out of water that passes through some part of their body

species: a very specific group of living organisms

Note to readers: Some of these words may have more than one definition. The definitions above match how these words are used in this book.

Contents

Chapter 1: Diving into the Depths

Hi! My name is Dr. Ick.
And like my name hints,
I love all things that might
make other people say, "Ick!"
Strange sea creatures are
especially fascinating to me!

This is my good friend Sam.
He's not a big fan of icky, sticky,
or strange things. But that's okay!
Sea creatures live far away
from us in the ocean.

The ocean is a large body
of salt water that is divided into
five regions: the Pacific,
Atlantic, Indian, Arctic,
and Southern Oceans.

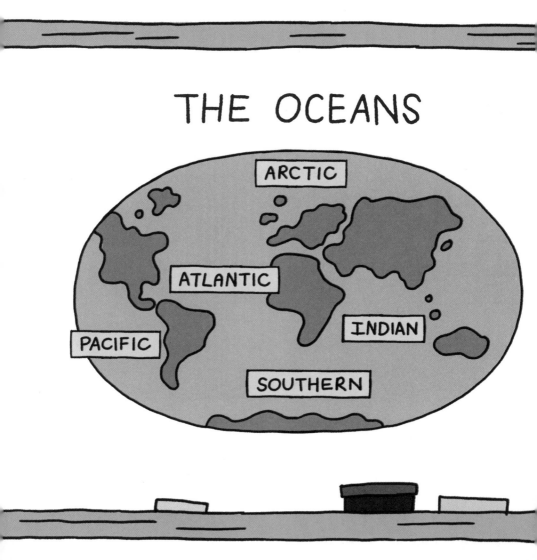

THE OCEANS

ARCTIC

ATLANTIC

PACIFIC

INDIAN

SOUTHERN

With tall mountains and
deep trenches, the ocean
has plenty of space for countless
fascinating sea creatures!

Some sea animals live in shallow water. Others prefer the deep, dark parts of the ocean.

The Japanese spider crab can be
found as deep as 1,640 feet
below sea level!

The deeper into the ocean we dive,
the stranger the animals we see.
These sea creatures must **adapt**,
or change, to suit the deeper water.

The ocean's depths are divided into five zones. Each zone has a distinct **ecosystem**, or network of living organisms and their environment.

The vampire squid lives in the mesopelagic (meh-zuh-puh-LA-jik) zone, where the water is almost completely dark.

But this **species**, or specific kind of organism, doesn't drink blood. They capture food particles on their tentacles.

When threatened, they expel a **bioluminescent** (say: bie-oh-loo-muh-NEH-sunt), or light-filled, substance into the dark water to confuse their predators.

Chapter 2:
The Wacky, Weird, and Wonderful

The ocean holds 99 percent
of Earth's **biosphere,** or parts
of Earth where life can exist.
However, humans have only explored
about 20 percent of the entire ocean.

That means there are many
strange species that have not been
discovered yet!

But one amazing species that has been discovered is the oarfish. Oarfish are thin and silvery and can reach up to 35 feet long.
That's similar in length to a school bus!

It's no wonder that sailors
thought these creatures
were sea monsters.
But oarfish are **filter feeders**,
with small mouths and no teeth.

Sea creatures come in all
different shapes and sizes.
Some are long and thin.
Some are round and . . . mushy.
Like the . . . blobfish!

The blobfish has a jelly-like body
that helps it float across
the ocean floor.
The blobfish's body becomes
"blobby" outside of the water
because there is less pressure
on land than in the deep sea.

You know that fish can swim,
but did you know that some
fish can walk?
The red-lipped batfish doesn't
walk on land. It has fins that help it
walk along the seafloor!

Do they go on
walks like me?

But that isn't the only unique
thing about this fish.
Like its name suggests,
the red-lipped batfish has
a pair of bright red lips!

Chapter 3: Masters of Disguise

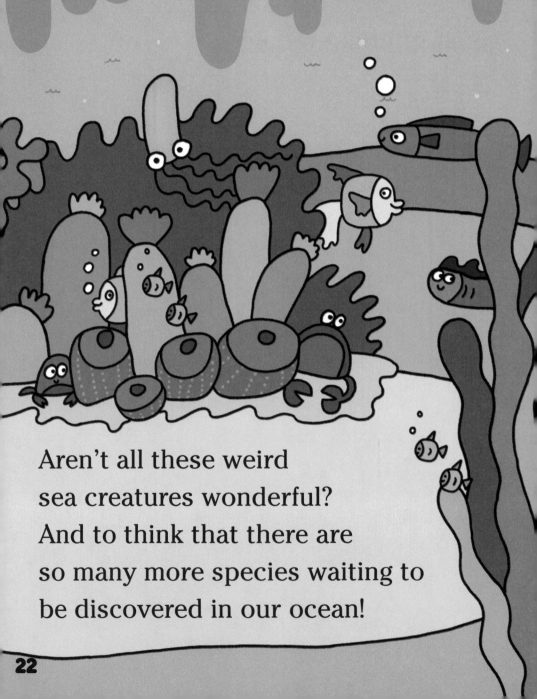

Aren't all these weird
sea creatures wonderful?
And to think that there are
so many more species waiting to
be discovered in our ocean!

Perhaps one reason why it can be challenging to discover new sea creatures is because some animals are masters of disguise!

One camouflaged creature,
the frogfish, is hiding
right there. Can you see it?

Found it!

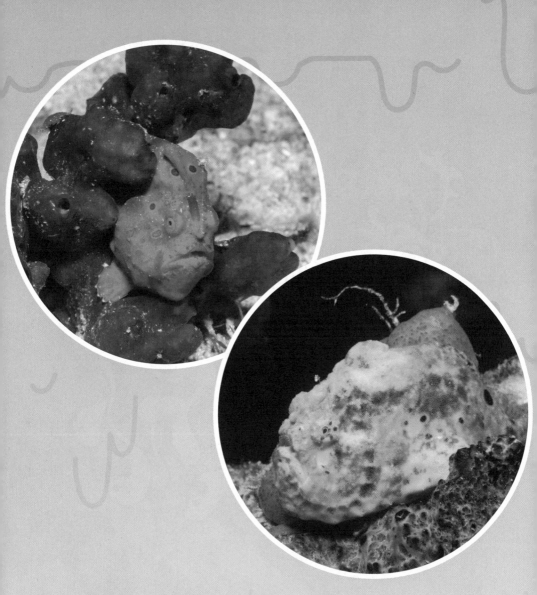

Frogfish come in different colors
and textures that help them
blend into their environment.
Some can have bright colors
to hide in coral reefs.
Others can look like rocks!

Sea creatures don't just hide
among coral and rocks.
Some like to hide in plants!

The leafy sea dragon has fins
that look like seaweed.
It avoids predators by
camouflaging itself in seagrass.

Fish aren't the only
sea creatures that can hide.
The mimic octopus is one
of the animals most talented
at hide-and-seek.

It's a fish! It's a
snake! It's an . . .
octopus?

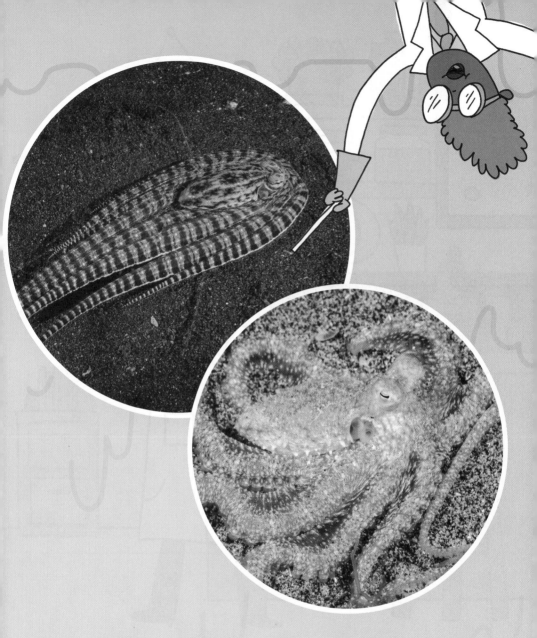

The mimic octopus can change
the color and texture of its skin
to avoid predators.
It can mimic sea snakes,
lionfish, flatfish, and more.

We've seen everything from
sea creatures as long as
school buses to fish that
can walk with their fins.

But there is still so much of
our ocean that we haven't seen.
Let's protect our oceans so future
explorers like you can discover
more wonderful creatures of the deep!

Create a Sea Creature!

There are countless sea creatures in the ocean waiting to be discovered. Maybe you will be the one to discover them someday! What do you think they will look like? In this activity, create a sea creature you think might be in the ocean.

You will need:

- a grown-up to help you
- different-colored paper
- scissors
- paint and a paintbrush
- glue
- crayons and/or markers

1. Draw a picture of your sea creature. Does it have tentacles or fins? How big is its mouth? Can it change colors?

2. Cut out your sea creature with the help of a grown-up.

3. Decorate your sea creature with strips of colored paper, crayons, markers, and paint!